Eat the Dirt Endorsements

If you dig poems or you don't I suggest you
read these poems from Heather because there are bits and pieces
of words and phrases in them like FUTILE SUCKING and SHE WAS GOD
and DOWN YOUR CHEEKS AND INTO THE DIRT
and A CASCADE OF FACES and ANOTHER DARK SLEEP
and I AM SO COLD and THE SUN DYING IN THE SEA and
A SPLEEN FULL OF BLOOD and EVERYTHING IS SPILLING
and DO THE BIRDS GET BORED? and THE STARS HAVE BEEN
   EXTINGUISHED
and a PATIENT MALVOLENCE which all together over all these pages
feel like life feels like because they're dirty and serene and angsty
and wondering and tender and feisty and loud and quiet and resilient
and all together they make you feel more alive which is such a
gift Heather is giving us here.

> **Rob Bell**, author of *New York Times* bestseller *Love Wins*

When we reach the dead end of what can be said in prose, that's when the secret passage of poetry may appear. The poetic gives the possibility of speech to the previously ineffable. And that is what I find in the God-saturated poems in *Eat the Dirt*. Heather Hamilton is a gifted poet exploring the greatest of mysteries.

> **Brian Zahnd**, author of *The Wood Between the*
> *Worlds: A Poetic Theology of the Cross*

Eat the Dirt, as its title suggests, is a deeply grounded collection. This is not poetry that flies off into abstraction or offers some thin disembodied light as compensation for the dark messiness of our lives. Instead, the poems in this fine collection venture down the dark descent and seek the light that's buried deep, the light of encounter rather than escape, 'the light of life born in a manger.' These are poems that, in the poet's own words, 'come up through your heart/from somewhere dark and deep at the center of it all.'

> **Malcolm Guite,** Poet, Priest, and Author

Even if you don't consider yourself a lover of poetry (yet), Heather Hamilton's new collection of poems will show you what poetry can do: using a few words to take you to moments of insight beyond words.

Brian D. McLaren, Author of *Life After Doom* and *The Last Voyage*

For the past 25 years, I have been counseling people through their religious deconstruction process and supporting their path of cultivating a more authentic and liberating non-religious spirituality. I wish I'd had Heather Hamilton's profound work of poetry, *Eat the Dirt,* to offer. Each of her 52 poems is a pathway into a more honest, courageous, and unshackled relationship with oneself and life. Poetry invites you into places where no systematic theology can go, and Heather Hamilton's *Eat the Dirt* are verses that open insights you won›t encounter in pop-spirituality writings or seminary books.

Jim Palmer, Founder of The Center for Non-Religious Spirituality, Author of *Inner Anarchy*

Poetry is the use of language to speak a different one. Where language inevitably reveals its fundamental lack, poetry takes its limitation and imbues it with a quiet presence that words, alone, cannot. The best word I have for this gift is *soul*— which is to say: connection—and the felt sense of it, somehow reintroducing us to ourselves as touchable. *Eat The Dirt* did that for me. In a world where so many of the words we have are used as divisive, or violent, or protective, what a gift it is, indeed, to receive this heart as open, as inviting, as vulnerable. It is an enormous risk—to give oneself away to the world—but what a bittersweet delight to hear the sound of that emptying. Heather's poetry… *sings.*

Levi Macallister *(Levi the Poet)*, Spoken-word artist and author

Heather's poetry is a visceral meditation on the ache and wonders of life. *Eat The Dirt* moves seamlessly between grief and a longing for transcendence, never shying away from the dark nights of the soul, nor losing sight of the hope that keeps us pressing on. Highly recommended.

Stephen Roach, host of the *Makers and Mystics podcast*, author of *Naming the Animals: An Invitation to Creativity*

Life can't be written. It must be lived. Moments and emotions cannot be articulated. They must be felt. Yet if we must try to write and if we must attempt to articulate all that encompasses our experiences in this one magical, alchemic, and achingly beautiful life then perhaps Heather Hamilton has done it with her book of poems, *Eat the Dirt*. So often it is impossible to find the right words to speak of our existence, the depth of feeling flowing through us, the profundity of the abyss that stares at us each day with its innate challenge to live into it, past it, in spite of it. Yet that is what poetry is for. To invite us into our lives in ways that are alive, ever-changing, multi-dimensional, and transformational. We count on poetry to do what prose cannot. And when it comes to Heather's work, she has somehow given us a poetic feast full of upsides that are down, paradoxes untold, honestly at all expense, simplicity and authenticity with no pretense or posturing. Yet all the proof of the personal we so hope our poets offer. Read only if you want to be seen. Approach only if you want to take an adventure inside yourself; if you want to laugh, cry, question, and imagine. This poet has not only lived to tell but has lived to trust. That somehow the story of her poetry speaks of calls to those who can't always find the words themselves. Come to the table with Heather's new book, *Eat the Dirt*.

Dr. Maria Francesca French, Author of *Safer Than the Known Way* and *Reconfiguring*

Heather Hamilton's poetry evokes my feelings and insights I would likely not otherwise have. I enter a theologically enchanted world with rich reservoirs. I recommend this book to those who want to feel and think anew!

Thomas Jay Oord, Author of *Open and Relational Theology*, *God Can't* and other books

Heather Hamilton's *Eat the Dirt* is one of the most moving collections of poetry I've ever read. Her words are raw, tender, and deeply human. It's as if she cracked her heart open and invited us to do the same. There's something sacred about the way she writes. It's honest without being harsh, soft without being vague. It holds you while also asking you to take a long, brave look at your own story. The poem "Winter" absolutely wrecked me—in the best way. I felt so seen in those lines, like Heather had reached into a part of my experience I hadn't fully put words to yet. That's what she does so beautifully throughout this book: she names the ache and the hope, the grief and the grit. She gives language to the seasons of life we tend to move through quietly, alone. But after reading her poetry, you don't feel so alone anymore. This isn't just a book of poems. It's an invitation to feel deeply, heal slowly, and to honor the parts of ourselves we usually try to hide. *Eat the Dirt* reminded me that there's beauty to be found even in the most unexpected places. I'm so grateful Heather wrote this. It's a gift for us all.

Leslie Nease, Podcast host of *Honoring the Journey*,
Author, Life and Faith Transitions Coach

Eat the Dirt

52 Poems on God and Being Human

By
Heather Hamilton

Cover Design: Rafael Polendo
Interior Illustrations: Achmad Nuryawan
Formatting: Nicole Jones Sturk

Hardcover: 978-1-968136-29-1
Paperback: 978-1-968136-02-4
Ebook: 978-1-968136-01-7
Audiobook: 978-1-968136-03-1

Printed in the United States of America

Library of Congress Cataloguing-in-Publication Data
Eat the Dirt: 52 Poems on God and Being Human / Heather Hamilton

For my steadfast friends—alive and gone.
You have made this life
bearable
and brilliant
and beautiful for me.

———————

I have changed my mind a thousand times
And you do not leave
What a gift it is to have a friend

In Love,
Heather

Contents

Foreword

My earliest memories involve my family of seven spread out in various places across our front driveway, watching as I drove my red tricycle toward the corner of the block.

Our house sat one door down from a quiet intersection—a modest ranch-style home painted in what some might call pea green or maybe olive green. Either way, I wouldn't recommend the color any more than I'd recommend the foods that inspired the colors, but what I *would* recommend, especially if you're a four-year-old with a trike, is a long, sloping driveway like ours. It served to be a great place to learn about speed, though a terrible place to learn about slowing down long enough to navigate corners.

The memories don't form a neat sequence; rather, they exist as overlapping impressions, a Gaussian blur of furious pedaling, squeaky wheels, wind rushing through hair, the corner approached with dangerous confidence, and the inevitable crash. I was fine. The ride was fine. Everyone was fine. There's nothing dramatic to report, well, except for the dramatic way the remainder of the memory plays out in slow motion: lying on the pavement, looking sideways, up and across the lawn, my family moving toward me with a mixture of laughter and concern, ready to dust me off and send me careening down the driveway toward the turn once more.

How could anyone calculate what it means for a boy to experience such acceptance? To gain validation amid failure? To pedal away from the warmth of home only to realize, albeit in a limited four-year-old way, that the warmth was there all along?

Goodness, what a gift.

Strangely, some fifty years later, Heather's writing prompted me to think about all of this ... about attempts and failures, scrapes and hugs, acceptance and warmth ... but upon reflection, perhaps it's not that strange, for what I read between the lines in *Eat the Dirt* is writing that comes from a similar place. It is, I've come to believe, one of the hallmarks of healthy psycho-spiritual development; that is, rather than the pressure to behave in a way that earns acceptance, that we all, in fact, are *already accepted.*

To adapt what Heather writes, this is the difference between "moving with the fire of the flame one feels inside," or needing to find something on the outside to light that flame. Unfortunately, much Western religion has conditioned us to think that God is out there somewhere, but God isn't *out there.* God's *in here.* The light always comes from the inside.

I wish I could tell you that the inside light causes life to go in an easy direction, but that's not the case. At least, it hasn't been with me. The early and relatively minor pain of trike spills turned into later and much more intense pain of deaths and murders, fires and diseases, betrayals and excommunications. What a crazy, dark, at times, debilitating journey it's been. To lose what was lost in each of those experiences, in a very real sense, was to lose a part of myself. I had been made in relationship *to* and *with* these things. When they died, a part of me died.

What's true for me is true for all of us and it is, in so many words, the very thing I suspect Heather is wrestling with when she stands in the ocean with her children and watches the "sun dying in the sea," for the truth is, the sun; that is, that thing or those things we've oriented our life around are always changing, fading, and dying. Which means *we* are always changing, fading, and dying. This is worthy of our attention and something to grieve.

And also, this is something to celebrate, for if everything is undergoing this process of change, then even death itself might be changing. Inspired by something similar, one biblical poet wrote that when Christ "embraced death, taking it into himself, he destroyed the enemy's hold on death and freed all who cower through life, scared to death of death." The implications are endless, but maybe none more important than this: you and I, and everything around us, can be made new.

Goodness, what a gift.

In other words, don't give up. The light is not conditioned upon experience, even when the experience is death itself; no, the light has always been and always will be with you. And if this is true—Oh, I hope that it is—I have nothing more to teach you about your life. (And you have nothing else you need ... except to read *Eat the Dirt*.)

—Jonathan J. Foster, Author of *indigo: the color of grief*

eat the dirt

I walked out into the forest
expecting to do the things I usually do
look up to see the sunlight cutting through the trees
closing my eyes to hold my face towards the ray

my heart soars underneath the canopy of trees
a cathedral made of beauty itself
my eyes follow the trunks all the way down
until suddenly my feet remember the ground beneath them
and I feel an incredible urge:

eat the dirt

I am overcome by desire
to savor God on my tongue
to swallow the crude taste
and stomach the ground
that grew me

to digest my disgust
raw and robust
and metabolize sediment and debris
I want to fill my belly
full of the All in All

dust to dust
God as bitter as earth
Life on the inside of me
God as sweet as honey
I want to eat it All

The Lord's Prayer

Most sacred One who holds, and flows through, and lives deep
    with us   .
Your Presence is the most precious thing in our hearts
Make what has always been known within us since the beginning
Manifest in our lives
Make who we are on the outside
Match who we are on the inside
Let us be present, Here and Now
Trusting that what we need will come to us at the right time
Give us courage to forgive ourselves and others
So we do not block the flow of Love with resentment
Help us to examine our hearts closely and honestly
So our perceptions are clear and we can do what is right
Let Your Love become our Life
Let us experience the vitality of Your Life animating us
Let Your glow of Love radiate from within us to others
Ground us in the eternal Now, which is infinitely deeper
    than time
Yes

the face of Jesus

sometimes when I sit on the porch
and listen to the wind blowing between the tree branches
and hear the light drizzle hitting the roof
I think about who I'd want to see when I die—
if I had to pick just one person
I feel like I should say Jesus
      everyone says Jesus, right?
but if I'm being honest, I'd pick you
because even though you've been gone for years
your Love still crosses space and time to hold me
      every once in a while
you made me be still when you were here
you bring me back to stillness when I picture you now
I think you fought to stay with me in the end
I told you all about how God answered my prayers for you to stay—
I just knew He'd heard all my protesting
but now I think it wasn't God who heard my begging
      I think it was you.
I think you willed your frail, thin body to live just a bit
  longer for me
until finally one day you screamed in so much pain that I
  gave up your ghost—
      Enough.
you waited for me to say yes—
      and then you left
when I need you, you return
the feeling of warmth on my cheeks where you used to hold
  my face
now in my dreams
and when you've guided me through, you leave
I never know when the coming or going will be
but it's always at just the right time
      if I had to pick: Jesus or you?
      I'd pick you
maybe, just maybe
      I'm picking the same One

no flying today

```
when I was a little girl
I wanted to fly
so one day I crossed the monkey bars
back and forth I swung
I was doing it!
...until I wasn't
I can't breathe
I can't breathe

staring up at the sky from the ground
on my back, gasping
shocked and dazed
unable to speak
no flying today

a teacher picks me up
and carries me like a bird
          she was God

now I am a mother
and one day I walk into the big box—
baby in arms
it's raining outside and the floors are slick...
I can't breathe
I can't breathe

staring up at the ceiling from the ground
on my back, gasping
shocked and dazed
unable to speak
no flying today

a man kneels down
and hands me a waiver to sign
he was church

I found faith
learning how to breathe
with my back on the cold, hard ground
looking at my own blood
while someone who needs me to be okay screams
no flying today
```

genesis 1

let us make man in our image
heavenly father
mother nature
wedded together
a sacred marriage
the two become one flesh
father and mother braided together
out of the two, I am born
taking refuge in her bosom
there's not a safer place to be
even father bows when she rages
for every wise man lets the woman have her say in things
and everyone knows that God's wrath rips through
Mother's fury

Embers in Eden

perhaps the hell I've always feared
was burning inside of me?
and the only way to heaven
was falling forward through the fire

sparked by grace, my soul ignites
mind and heart engulfed in heat
I've made a mistake
let me drift back to sleep

give me the inferno I thought was heaven
the combustion I called love
take me back to entertaining
the fantasies I dreamed of

this pain is suffocating
my life bursting into flames
writhing in the violent death
of everything I knew burning down

but as smoke begins to clear
grey ash settles on the ground
I dust off a brilliant diamond
at last, I am found

the Secret Garden of my longing
just past the flaming sword
a blaze of truth cut through the deadwood
until finally I was free

now embers are extinguished
Eden's earth has finally cooled
the Tree of Life stretched up to heaven
casting shadow-streets of gold

Mother!

the God-sized hole in my heart
is shaped like a mother
whose dark eyes burn through me
whose breath suffocates me
whose arms swallow me
whose mouth pierces my soul and
sucks the very life blood out of me

wiry fingers sharp as shards
jetting out of the black abyss
my heart is gripped from inside out
a web I can't untangle

futile sucking for a taste of gold
milk and honey wasted in the mouths of men
my lips dry and cracked
yearning for just one drop on my tongue
left with my own tears to quench my thirst

my cries quelled with laughter
with rage
with drama
with drugs
with sleep
with silence
with betrayal

please don't give me jesus
please no barren savior with hairy chest and scratchy beard
no blood-stained loin cloth
no bleeding hands
no dirty feet
I can't bear to pretend to enjoy the embrace of filth

when hellfire burns up my heart
the flames that fill the void will scream:

Mary!

monsters

I cannot look at you
you are not striving like I am
to be good
I see a monster in you

it is ugly and deformed
I hate it and wish it dead
I've strived my whole life
to be good

after all those years of striving
of striving to be good
I saw a reflection of myself in you
I saw a monster in me

I am you
and you are me
and we are both monsters
I know this now

the virgin birth

depression's darkness stretching across the sky
a rolling cloud casting infinite shadow
looking up, searching for a ray of gold
knocking, knocking, knocking on doors in the inn
a chance to stay above ground and bask in sunlight again

hope eclipsed, all doors are closed
no room up above for what's to be born
conceived from within
buried deep in dark earth
held in the virgin womb of untouched soul

Light of Life born in the manger
where the outside world does not want to go
and does not think to look for anything sacred
deep in the heart
human born divine

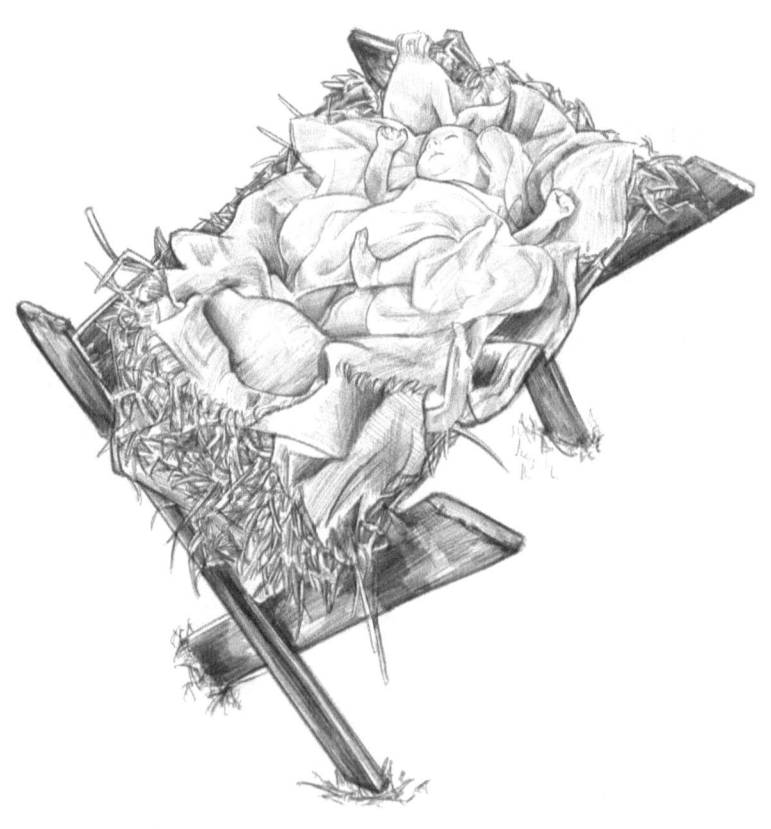

the grief circle

there's this circle called grief
where you can come and sit
and you don't get kicked out because
someone thinks they had it worse than you
(and it's really important to them that they had it worse
   than you)
in this circle, you belong
even though we wish we didn't
everyone touches the tears of God
      now or later
they come up through your heart
from somewhere dark and deep at the center of it all
down your cheeks and into the dirt
they warm the earth for you to lie down in it
this circle does not see your riches or rags
only skin and bones
      come sit down with those of us who know

forgive

you think any wrong can be made right?
    no, no, no.
you don't understand.
nothing that needs forgiven can ever be undone.
it cannot be made right.
    it is only the unforgiveable that needs forgiveness!
when the wound delivers you into the ultimate release—
that is Redemption.
and you know you would never have received the gift without
    the wound.
    you are finally okay with how it all really is.
    Forgive.
so you can live your life.
    if it feels too hard, that's right.
    if you can't, stay with it longer.
keep looking into the dark.
keep looking into the dark.
look harder—you become the light that fills the darkness.
look harder—the light of God pierces through dark.
look harder—your eyes become windows through which God sees.
    when you see, you understand.
    when you understand, there is nothing left to forgive.
the light within you is brighter than the darkness of what
    happened.
and you would have never come to know that, unless what
    happened—
    Happened.

where is God?

pregnant with Life
I looked down
to my surprise
I found a child inside

a little light
that needed me
I could not hear before
but I can now

a promise to protect
at all costs
even until the end
even when God can help me no longer

if I can manage to give you a little peace, my child
perhaps I will feel it as well
a space that we share inside of me
a peace no one else but us can hear

everything that never was

```
one day it suddenly hit me
everything that could have been,
        that wasn't
all the paths I could have taken,
        but didn't
all the possibilities that arrived too late
wondering if maybe I'll find you earlier the next time around
this too is grief
```

the sign of Jonah

don't go out searching for suffering
it will find its way to you all on its own
and when it does
you'll want to leap to resurrection
        heed this:
if you try to stay up
        the longer the down will be
that's the truth, I'm afraid
because suffering will insist on the down
and it will win that wrestling match—
        trust me
(perhaps you'll need to find that out for yourself)

when you suffer—
        and you will
and God seems to vanish
suffer in the right way—
with all your heart
all your mind
all your strength
fixated on your Beloved
who lives in the Secret Place
        inside of you

when you suffer—
don't worry about reaching up
        worry about going down with God
and then there will be nowhere
you are afraid to go

        if you can trust the deep dive down
the "up" will take care of itself

a bright sadness

I have seen a thousand
tragedies I cannot unsee
a thousand fates
        that make me shudder
the kinds of scenes that make me
disbelieve and cling to belief
        in the same breath
my imagination runs wild with ideas
I never wanted to know
and still, when my children look up at me
so innocently
and harken all the joy in my heart
I know there is good in the world
        a bright sadness will suffice
as a way to travel through

the boy who died

I once knew a mother whose little boy died
for years and years, she would ask
      why God didn't save her son
where was God?
where was God?
she could never stop crying
      even when she was not crying
      she was crying
where was God?
where was God?
I will tell you where God was
      God was crying for her son who died
wondering why he had to die that way
wondering why it has to be this way
crying and crying
      not up there, but in Here
Here, living through unbearable suffering
Here, crying for her children
      Here, doing what she can to make it better

judgement day

when I die
I know I will see God's face
        yes
my mother
my father
my sister
my brother
my children
my friends
my enemies
the one I loved
the ones I hated
myself
        the light bursting out of broken vessels
                the eye of Eternity
        a cascade of faces
collapsing into God

only the most beautiful things will do

you must trust the people
who have suffered through the darkest of nights
who have lived through hell and somehow glisten
who still insist on Beauty
and Joy
        these are the souls who do not have time for games
or fantasies
or false hopes
for them, only what is real will suffice
you are wise to follow
in the direction that they point

the cross

yesterday I was elated
full of life
today
numb
I can barely move
what's the point?
the waves rise and crash
over and over and over
all the striving—for what?
how I yearn to be full of joy once again
to have all the blessings in the world
yet I still long to lie down and go to sleep
       I am crossed with the opposites
unable to move
while my heart bleeds out
suspended in a frozen animation
of death
and longing
and stillness
and the terror of true silence—
       Lord, have your way with me.

winter

I brace myself for the cold snap
the first sign that Mother is about to hide
and I will be left alone to endure the fading
of everything I love

all the warmth and light that draws me out of myself
now receding
and so am I

I smile

but a silent scream within me
feels my soul descending
into another dark sleep

I know I will feel Mother's warmth again
but can I bear the wait this year?
only time will tell

I am so cold

the cage of hope

I crouched down in the rain
and let the water baptize me
I screamed and screamed
until my nerves blew out
        and my voice rose above my cage of shame
I could finally tell you the truth
if you only knew, I thought—
you would help me
        you didn't help because you didn't know
        you didn't help because you didn't know
I said the words

you denied—
Adam's shame
you hid—
Adam's blame

        you knew
        you knew

and you looked the other way

when you broke my heart
you broke my chains
the truth that set me free:

        I was always on my own

the dark

the stars have been extinguished
and suddenly I cannot see
the darkness
the darkness
so barren
so full of emptiness
as I feel my way around
for something warm and alive
the farther I reach out
the heavier the collapse into my chest
until I know—without a doubt—
I am alone
there's nothing left to do
but open my eyes
and look into the dark
and say yes to this terrible—liberating—
aloneness

Cinderella

arms open
a naïve girl expecting embrace
                the confusion creeps
        and recedes
perhaps the effort—this time—
will open the locked door
over and over again she tries
                an earnest goodness
        a rejected beauty
sits in a heap of grey ash
soot-stained clothing
now fodder for scorn
writhing in bewildered frustration

        still, unjaded enough
to smile at trees
        at squirrels
                at leaves
        another try
                another bid to connect
a sincere excitement—

        and the ire is drawn
        the rats are unleashed
the girl is banished, once again
        to her pile of ash behind the locked door

Love wasted on what never could be
        tears carry away her innocence
                until all that's left is a choice
                        a future only fit for her
                                a yes to the golden slipper

it's time to go now.

the cave

for years I wandered
in what seemed like a dark cave
my hand stretched out
looking for yours

time after time
it felt like I would brush against you
my heart would leap
hoping now we could finally begin

each time was amiss
still in the dark
I stood confused
wondering why I couldn't find you

my hand stretched out
yours was too
my hand stretched out
        yours too, right?

another day, more dark wandering
sudden pain struck my hand
and I realized there was never a hand
reaching out for mine

        only a mouth waiting to bite

I walked out of the dark cave
and never looked back
I have no regret
other than the time I spent
trying to touch
a hand that was not there
        and all the words I gave you
in the dark

hunted

my head is suddenly spinning
I feel a cold chill cascade down my body
I cannot remember how I got home
it was the moment I abruptly knew—
I was being hunted
      the years of odd interactions
came flooding back to memory
how had I not put this together before?
      but now, it is all I can see
you are the predator
I am the prey
even though I cannot see you
      I can feel your eyes.
without a hand laid on me
I am invaded
knowing you are watching me
you are nowhere and everywhere
      a shadow full of darkness
      a black vigil I can't escape

a spleen full of blood

I shudder at the moment that I knew—
the general had narrowed
and I had become the particular

I dipped into a shadow
and attempted to shake off your gaze
but you held me in your mind's eye

I could feel you fixated on me

a patient malevolence
I saw your spleen full of blood
in my dreams

there are only two choices now—
shrink
or look back at you

the lake of ice

the descent into hell
it was hot, to be sure
burning off everything
unworthy of Paradise

something that surprised me
that preachers got wrong
the bottom wasn't hot—
but a frigid block of ice

the devil stone cold
encased in a frozen tomb
dead but alive
too brittle to move

if frostbitten lips of betrayers
could manage to speak
they would beg for some heat
to melt misery

a fiery inferno?
a welcomed mercy—
to thaw this lake of ice
where silent screams cannot escape

no preacher told me about this place
where cold hearts stay still
they never beat
and never burn

the cold box with a glass window

this room is sterile
white walls and right angles
a box in the wild—
          a wild I cannot seem to touch
with hands and face pressed against a glass window
I feel the heat
I'm drawn to what I can see out there
          longing to be tossed around by it
                    but encounter eludes me

somewhere deep within
I have a memory of what once was
          before I became trapped in this impotent place—
this cold box with a glass window

surely this coffin will suffocate me
cradle to grave—
a box of death
but still,
I look out the glass window
          and pray grace will one day take me in

ambivalence

at the center of all
and nothing
which way do I go?
frozen by choices
        and each one fatal
to go this way
feels like the death of things
to go that way
        death too
still and stuck
centered between everything I cannot put down
pushed and pulled all at once
time and time again
I look out everywhere
I go nowhere

the burning bush

day in and day out
I walk the same path
the same faceless faces
pass me by

I smell the same scents
hear the same sounds
round and round
time cast the die

but every so often—
I catch a flicker of light
glistening
out of the corner of my eye

and everything would be easier
        had I never turned my head

the cathedral

    standing in the sunlight
    beaming through stained glass

            in the background—
    the sound of tourists' shutters snapping pictures

    is this sanctuary or museum?
    alive or relic?
    the body is dead
    but the spirit of what was—
    what maybe still is?
            it draws me in

    I look up
    pondering if anyone was ever raptured in this place?
    and if they sang out
    or stayed silent?
    my heart is loud
            I wonder if anyone can hear it?

    I leave as quietly as I entered

home

I once left home for a very long time
I saw beautiful places
ate wonderful food
touched handsome people
and felt an emptiness grow in my belly—
a longing for my soil
        to bathe in it
to feel its coarseness on my palms
on my soles
to put it in my mouth
and feel home coat my throat
and fill my stomach
and plant me in the heart of the earth
        with roots so deep
they touch the other side

birds

do the birds get bored?
in between their flights
from branch to branch
the liminal time spent perched on a limb
somehow does not seem wasted
        yet, I am not a bird
I watch them and they help me sit still
but after a while
I itch again with existential dread:
        what am I to do here?
the boredom frustrates me
and throws me towards madness
oh, to be a bird!
        and not feel like such a waste
every once in a while
I seem to catch a glimpse—
a clue into why I'm here
        it feels so specific
        yet elusive
I fear one day I may see it
and the regret of not seeing it sooner
        will send me falling from my branch

longing

I cannot go to sleep
I'm staring at the moon
thinking about a life I never lived
wondering what might have been
if my fickle heart had had its way
I guess I'll never know
I dream my dreams lying awake
          they pull me in to play
                    but sometimes I can't escape
now which world is it I'm living in?
am I asleep or am I awake?

failure

I think—no,
I'm pretty sure I'm going to fail
and this is not going to work
but hell
I'm going to do it anyway
because I cannot get it out of my mind
and at least I'll feel alive
if I try

sun heart

the sun shone so bright in you
riding the line between ecstasy and hell
cursing boredom and despair
you burned brilliantly
I could never quite keep up

I remember the night
you drove past my home
one thousand miles closer to me than you usually were
still not close enough
never time to stop

you sped on by me
                my heart felt yours go by
and I wished you would stop
I begged you to stop
little did I know
that was the closest we'd be again
little did I know that you wanted to die
        or did you?
                maybe not.
but either way—

you laid down and said no
all the fire inside you
turned in on itself so quickly
internal combustion and a gun
only has one outcome

the blazing heart yearns to bleed
        and it better—
        and it better.
or the body will

drowning my dreams

I do not recall anyone telling me
how sad it is to grieve a dream
that I am suffocating in my own hands

holding it underwater
as it wrestles me relentlessly
struggling for another gulp of air

my dream is slowly dying
I can feel its life draining out
rolling down my cheeks

a strange happening in the woods

the woods have shown me
a thousand things or so
secrets, really—
that I cannot speak in the village

at first, I was angry
I was angry that they were angry
don't you remember?
it's Me!

but understand—you must understand—
that a strange thing happened out there
        a very strange thing, indeed
I cannot be angry forever
that the village does not understand

little by little, over time
lights flicker in the village
one day, maybe—every knee
until then, grace upon grace

neat lines

my suspicion is that
your whole life has been
boxes and buildings
and you have not yet let nature disturb
all your neat lines
        and why would you?
it's chaos, in fact
and you know that deep down
        so why would you?
but something in you craves chaos
        and wild
                and an experience to awaken
                        your fire
        and assure you that you are part of it

the business of trees

how many more times
will I get to look up
and see these towering trees
with wings reaching up to the heavens?

the world has gone mad
this I know
but look!
have you seen these trees?

you are not neglecting
your duty to the world
when you give yourself
a moment of peace

can you hear it?
the rain is pouring down
ricocheting off
infinite leaves

come and sit a little while
and ponder this other world
that sings its song
and does not ask permission

all the acorn's fates

I look at this acorn and wonder—
it seems to have no problem with waiting
does it know the potential hidden inside of itself?
either to bloom or to be smashed to bits

I gather I have much to learn from this seed,
accepting of all the fates
willing to sacrifice itself in service of the One—
the only fate that Is

the multitude of possibilities inside of me
holler loudly in my mind:
are you ready to let go of what could have been?
no!

jealous am I of the acorn
who is blown around in the wind
with the peaceful assurance
that it will either bloom—

or find its rest in the dust again

saved by the chestnut tree

how long, Oh God
must I remain here?
caged like a bird
with wings unclipped
longing to fly

even in my bondage
you find me
a friend just outside the window
speaking to me
in my loneliness

each time you comfort me—
a bar of the cage comes off
though I haven't moved
and, in fact—
I have nowhere to go now

I wish to be right where I am
because you're here with me
the chestnut tree who never moves
who never leaves
I find Eternal Life—

right where I am
is where you are
and my heart is okay with it all
with how it is
with how it always was

the winepress

there hung a man
up on that tree
full of God
he suffered slow

just like the grapes
when time was ripe
God pressed on him
and took his time

the wrath of God
bearing down
royal red
began to flow

on my knees
I held my cup
and filled my body
full of wine

still hanging there
and emptied out
I looked at him
from down below

the broken skin
and taste of juice
bitter and sweet
I'm full of both

intoxicated now
with Life
his frame was crushed
so I could know

I heard the light

I woke up early one morning
before the sun came up
I noticed that the birds were singing
while the sky was still black
the birds sang in the dark
      and I could hear the light
before I could see it
      I could hear the light
before I could see

a real smile

when I look at you
I have this startling certainty
that I'm going to be okay
it doesn't quite make sense to me
that you wake up with a smile on your face
but nevertheless, you do
        I did not believe that people like you actually existed
until I saw you with my own eyes
day after day
morning after morning
before you have time to think, you smile
too quick to be fake
you finally convinced me that
        Joy exists on its own

tears of the past

let life heal you—
maybe even God
pry open each finger
        to see the past
        heavy in your palm
if you let it breathe a little
it won't leave you
but it will get lighter
and start to flow
and then the air of life can start to move through you—
        again
the sadness will be there
but so much more will be, too
you will be okay with the sadness then—
maybe even thankful
        can you have a little faith
        that what I say is true?

a mountain to climb

a life worth living
needs a mountain to climb
"but not this one," I said
mine was not supposed to be this hard
forging my way up
as life collided time after time

the higher I climb
the more I can see
that every grip I found in the rock to hold
was a life before mine
buckling under pressure

I am standing on the shoulders
of what should not have been
yet, here I stand
a bow in reverence
for the rubble beneath my feet
and for those whose foundation
collapsed under the weight of their world—

they gave me this mountain to climb
and it's only from my peak
that I can see the splendor of the story
underneath me

everything is spilling

I am overwhelmed—and often
by the spirit that splashes around in me
and spills out from my heart and my eyes
I have tried so hard to be stoic—
to really be unmoved
instead of pretending there is not an ocean—
both calm and raging—sometimes all at once
within me
but after a while, I always fail
I cannot tell if others appreciate this spirit in me or not
it forever feels like too much
even for me
especially for me
in so many ways, the more it is alive
the more tired I become
and still,
this is the only way I know how to be—
the only way I have ever been
I have to believe
this spirit within me is the
possibility of God
and what a frightening possibility that is

the flame I feel inside

the most precious word in my heart is God
and I do not pretend to really know
what that even means
I know I have loved things
        that were not real
and dreamed dreams
that only existed in my imagination
I have held onto hope
        for possibilities that do not exist
                and never existed
but none of that matters
what matters is that
I loved
I dreamed
I hoped
I felt my heart
and that was real—
        whatever that means
existing, for me, is beholding
the beauty of the ineffable
and moving with the fire
        of the flame I feel inside

daddy's tears

tonight I heard my daddy cry
for the first time in my life
he's an old man now
and I had wondered for some time
if his tears were still there
        or if they had been buried too far down
to ever make the long journey back up
I was sad when I heard him
but strangely—
relief, too
I always suspected they were there
        waiting to be dislodged
what a gift, I feel—
to hold his tears
on this side of life

strewn across time

everything that happened
all the memories
strewn across the surface of time
tossed around
up and down

laid out
I find myself
depleted by this profanity—
time.

pulled deeper
underneath it all
I find a fount
where time finds its center

each moment
as it was the very first breath
born again
full of vitality

and me, too
at the beginning of time
with all my Life
Intact

the ocean's prayer

the best prayer I ever taught my children
was to stand in the ocean at sunset
for a few short minutes
and be still
they tried to chatter like children do
but I insisted

the kernels of sand tickled their little toes
as they bounced up and down with each wave of the water
    rushing past them
the giant orange globe demanding their eyes
for once, mama said it was okay to look straight at the sun

the closer the sun came to the horizon,
the more radiant it became
its moment of death the most beautiful
God seems to demand that we realize this
so that we can go on with our lives as they are meant to be
    lived

the sun dying in the sea
we belong to this mysterious dance
feet dug into the sand close enough to the shore
the water that could wreck us—mercifully does not
my children stand on the edge of being swallowed
trusting the safety of my arms
while we gaze at the dying fire together

if this prayer in the water washes over them—
Oh, I hope that it does!—
I have nothing more to teach them about their lives

Thank you for reading Eat the Dirt.
Your review will help other readers discover this book.
Please consider writing an honest review of the book
on the site where you purchased it.
I appreciate your help.

— **HEATHER HAMILTON**, 2025

Other works by Heather Hamilton
Returning to Eden:
A Field Guide for the Spiritual Journey

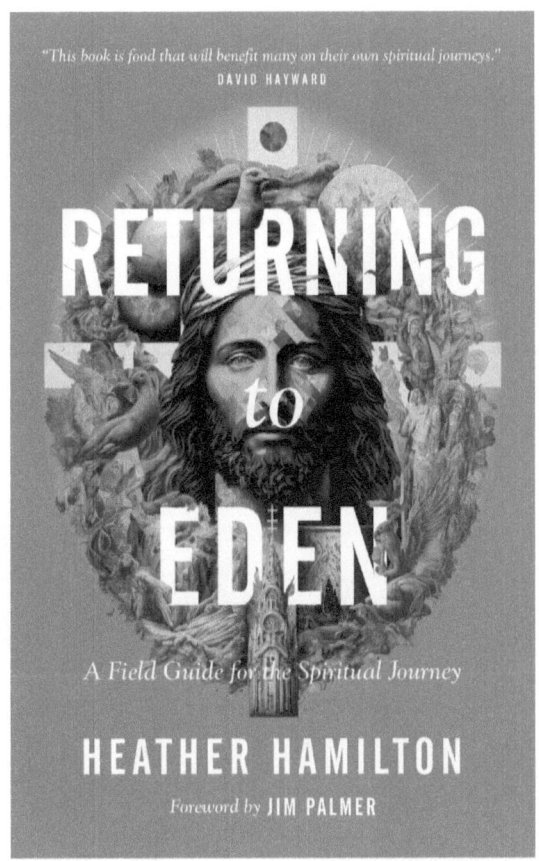

Excerpt from
Returning to Eden

Introduction

There's a comedic irony when salvation is found in your religion falling apart.

Growing up as an evangelical Christian, there was a notable emphasis in the church on sharing your personal testimony. This is the story of someone's conversion to Christianity. I used to bemoan my personal testimony because I found it rather boring. Though I still cringe a little to admit it, my vices in life are rooted in wanting to be special. Not ordinary. *Not boring.* I always felt a tinge of envy when someone would share a compelling story about how they became a Christian. Not having a very unique story, I unconsciously endeavored to be a special kind of Christian. I did this in the only way I knew how—*sincerity.* I was what the church called a "sold-out-for-Jesus" kind of Christian.

When I was seven years old, I attended a summer Vacation Bible School (VBS) at a Baptist church in Georgia. VBS is common in the American South. Churches offer week-long summer camps where kids play games, eat snacks, and learn about the Bible, while the parents get a break. At that young age, a pastor told me that there was a heaven and a hell. I was going to one of those places when I died. He explained that because I had sinned, God couldn't look at me or be with me anymore, because He hated sin so much. I was destined for hell where I would burn forever in agony. The worst part wasn't that my skin would be melting off, nor that I would never see my family again, but that I would be separated from God.

But there was good news! Because God is just and needs a payment of death for sin, Jesus came to die on a cross as a substitute payment. He rose from the dead to prove he was God's Son. I could trust that this pastor's message I was hearing about this cosmic arrangement was The Truth. Period. Hard stop.

If I just believed that this was all true and said aloud that I was a sinner who needed forgiveness, Jesus would come into my heart and save me from hell, and I would go to heaven when I died. When God looked up my name in the Book of Life, he wouldn't see me. He would see Jesus's name and blood covering my name. *(Somehow, I was simultaneously precious to God and also so abhorrent that He couldn't look at me.)*

Like any frightened seven-year-old hearing this would do, I prayed. I asked Jesus to come into my heart and decided to be baptized later that week. I remember being too small for any of the gowns the church had. So, I stood alone in the hall waiting my turn, swallowed up in a huge adult robe dragging the ground. I was baptized in front of hundreds of VBS kids, many of them peering over the glass into the pool. I was a small, earnest, sensitive child. The experience felt very noisy and chaotic. But I just wanted to be in God's family. To be with *my* family. To be loved and accepted. I didn't want to be unworthy of acceptance and love because I had lied to my mom that one time. Even that small sin committed in fear was enough for me to burn. I longed to be a good girl. But obviously, I was a bad girl. God created me and loved me. Yet, I didn't deserve God's love. I didn't deserve to be in His family.

When you are seven, you accept as true whatever grown-ups tell you. This specific paradigm of God—heaven and hell, plan of salvation, and eternity—was the foundation upon which I oriented the next twenty-five years of my life.

After I was "saved" through this initiation, my life's purpose became telling other people the "good news." On the elementary school playground, I told my schoolmates about heaven and hell and Jesus. At the ripe old age of twelve, I decided my calling was to be an overseas missionary. I slid tracts into the lockers at my high school. These little "gospel" pamphlets, usually illustrated with cartoons and Bible verses plucked out of context, offered a simple and persuasive formula for salvation. Some literally had "The ABCs of Salvation." I was too shy to just walk up to my peers and ask them if they had accepted Jesus into their heart. This lack of boldness bothered me, but I reasoned that a colorful gospel tract from an anonymous person would do the trick.

I went on mission trips in high school. For weeks I wore the same princess dress in Peru, performing a drama and "sharing the gospel" through a translator to hundreds of people on the street. Our group would roll up to a corner on a busy street—flash mob style—plug in the PA, and start our performance. I'm still not entirely sure what the drama actually communicated, but I got to do a backflip at one point in it, which hopefully wowed a few spectators to salvation. As silly as it sounds, this was a special time in my life. On these trips I particularly noticed how much genuine joy some of the poorest people seemed to have. It was a joy noticeably missing in the Christianity back home. Later, in my adult years, I worked shooting baptism testimony videos of kids. Curiously, I noticed that the majority of children telling their stories had a similar story as mine. Adults told them "the truth." Children believed it. Children grew up to become adults that tell more children "the truth." And the wheels on the bus go round and round.

I occasionally would muse over the good fortune I had to be born in America at the time that I was. After all, this "gospel" was bequeathed to me as a child. I also wondered about being born in a different part of the world at a time when this "truth" wasn't prevalent or easily accessible. In so many different scenarios, figuring out the formula to get to heaven would have required a great deal of effort, sacrifice, and suffering. "Thank God I didn't have to go through all that," I would think to myself at times. I just happened to live in a time and place in history where the truth was readily accessible. And yet, the stakes were so high. Eternal life was on the line. It didn't quite compute why God would make it so easy and obvious for myself and the people I loved and so difficult for others, but I was grateful.

My conversion to Christianity didn't feel special or unique. I couldn't control that. But I could control the sincerity and effort I put into being a devoted Christian. I wanted to lead people to Jesus. I didn't earn my salvation, but I could earn a "well done, good and faithful one" from God when I died. I strived to earn my stamp of divine approval. I wanted God to know that I took the mission seriously and gave it my all.

Not surprisingly, my zeal was rewarded by the evangelical church. I was continuously invited into circles of leadership. This trajectory continued, and by the time I was thirty, I had firmly established myself as a leader at a very large megachurch. My husband is a musician and had found our church to be a place where he could spread his wings musically and play with the best musicians in the city. Eventually, he became the music director leading a service for tens of thousands of people each week. We had written a good story that we were proud of, and it seemed God had blessed our efforts.

What happened next is what finally produced my not-so-ordinary story. A few weeks after I'd given birth to our third child and just before my thirty-third birthday, I experienced what could be conventionally labeled as a nervous breakdown. As unresolved traumas began surfacing, that led to terrifying episodes of PTSD, although I did not have the language to understand what was happening at the time. I began suffering waves of debilitating panic attacks and was overcome with hopelessness and despair. These episodes became increasingly severe and frequent. Over the course of a few days, they became constant to the point where I had lost control of my body. Nearly overnight, my life went from being the model of a well-behaved, successful, Christian, American woman, to someone whose underground anxiety had erupted like a volcano of spewing molten lava. Looking back, I realized I had suffered from anxiety since childhood. *But I couldn't even label the feeling because it was such a normal internal state. You can't know something is wrong if you've never known anything different.*

As I continued spiraling into more and more intense panic, I also had the inner knowing that what was happening to me was deeply spiritual. It felt as if I was dying. I was spiritually dying. I felt my soul descending deeper and deeper into an abyss of despair. As I wailed and begged God for help, for the first time in my life, I felt nothing. My soul felt absolute abandonment and alienation. The image of God I had carried with me was vaporized. In my most desperate hour, as I was crying out for God, *there was nothing*. No comfort. No presence. No nothing.

A few years earlier, my uncle had died by suicide. He had two children (my cousins) who loved him very much. It had been difficult for me to understand why someone would take their own life, especially when they leave behind people that love them. I have three children of my own, and any parent must know that their children will suffer when a parent takes their own life.

Perhaps one of the most frightening parts of my breakdown was a distinct moment when I realized: "I get it. I cannot live like this." I understood, for a moment, what my uncle might have felt. I was not imminently suicidal, but a sobering realization told me if I continued on like this much longer, it would get to that point very quickly. The complete absence of God in my desperation and despair was crushing to my soul. All light and hope had been eclipsed by this absence. Whoever I was calling out to was not there. *I was in hell.*

I knew at this point that my life was in danger. I mustered all the courage I had and whispered three words to my husband: "I need help." My husband called 911. A few minutes later, I opened the door to my house to find a transgender woman standing on my porch who had arrived to help me. She was part of the emergency response team. My first reaction to this was *fear*. Growing up as a Christian, I viewed myself as the rescuer. My fear came from years of a church background which perpetuated the idea that I was different from those in the LGBTQ population. That, in some way, they needed my rescuing. In my ignorance, I thought this was a loving, compassionate view. I was the one who was supposed to be helping "people like her." Not the other way around.

But suddenly, a palpable love began to emanate from this woman. There was something inside of me that immediately recognized this presence as Christ. It was an ineffable essence that was at once new and immediately familiar, like a feeling I'd suddenly remembered from another life. It was the most *real* moment I had ever experienced. The irony was not lost on me that I was a leader at this influential megachurch, but Jesus was standing on my porch in a body I would least expect to find him in.

In that sacred moment, Jesus flipped the table of my life.

Over the next several months, I had similar experiences as this one. Moments where I would suddenly feel an ineffable presence, as if my reality was suddenly saturated with a thick, benevolent texture. It reminded me a little of the liminal state between dreaming and waking—except I was completely alert, and my body was fully absorbing the energy of whatever or whomever was in my presence. I began to experience premonitions in my dreams where I'd foresee an interaction with someone and then later experience the interaction in real time. All of these moments had similar qualities to them, and my senses began to become familiar with the nature of these experiences.

Reflecting upon my life before this, I can identify a similar experience occurring the moment I gave birth to my first child, Norah.

It felt as though the perceivable intensity of heaven was emanating from inside of both me and my daughter, but also pressing out from us and pushing in on us at the same time. Like gravity pulling and grace lifting, such that I felt suspended in a capsule outside the boundaries of time. It felt like *eternity*.

After Norah was born, the window of that feeling slowly closed, and I associated that experience exclusively with childbirth. My mistake was attributing this experience of heaven with an external event (the birth of my daughter). In actuality, what had occurred was that my mind had become still long enough for my heart and body to *be here now* and sense my own soul. In reality, the experience came from within.

Following my encounter with the transgender woman who was channeling Christ on my front porch, this experience of the *eternal* was occurring often in very ordinary situations and had longevity and fluidity to it. It felt like a state of awareness that opened up and became fully available to me with greater frequency.

During this season of my life, I was becoming increasingly aware that many of the tenets of my evangelical faith no longer made sense. I was experiencing more and more cognitive dissonance between what I had been taught in church my whole life and what I was experiencing in real time along the everyday paths of life. Ironically, many Bible stories that had become rote over the years suddenly became fairly accurate and relevant metaphors to describe my experiences, which I later came to define as *mystical* experiences.

My personal encounters and spiritual revelations began to contradict much of what I was taught from an early age about God and the nature of reality. My evangelical theology required me to force pieces of the puzzle together that I knew no longer fit. My goal in this book is to offer a new paradigm through which to consider objective spiritual (and by extension, *natural*) laws. In my search to understand the nature of God, the universe, and humanity, I stumbled upon the study of biblical mythology and was struck by its accuracy in illuminating the lived human experience. It offered a precise diagnosis of the plight of the human soul and charted a map for spiritual growth and transformation. If the term "myth" throws you, hang tight—I'll dive into it in Chapter Four, *The Function of Myth*. It doesn't mean what you're afraid it does. If you'll stick with me, my hope is to lead you to a well of undiscovered potency hiding in the biblical stories that has the power to both revitalize your life and encourage your sharpest reasoning skills. The time has come for the heart, mind, and body to come fully alive. The world is yearning for a breakthrough beyond our well-worn religious tropes.

CHAPTER 1

The Christian of the Future

The Christian of the future will be a mystic, one who has experienced God for real, or he or she will not exist at all.[1]

—FR. KARL RAHNER (1904–1984)[2]

There is a profound story in part of the testimony of St. Francis of Assisi. Like many religious people, Francis experienced his religious group tribally and had an abhorrent fear of certain "outside" groups of people. For many Christians in the world today, that fear and disdain might be directed at LGBTQ+ persons, different religious groups such as Muslims or Hindus, or non-religious groups such as atheists and humanists. For Francis, his disdain was directed towards lepers, and he avoided them at all costs.

---

1. Karl Rahner, "The Spirituality of the Church and the Future," *Theological Investigations XX* (London/New York: Darton, Longman and Todd/Crossroad, 1961/1992), 149.

2. Fr. Karl Rahner (1904–1984) was an influential Jesuit priest and theologian from Germany.

One day while riding his horse, Francis encountered a leper with his hands out, asking for charity. His initial instinct was to turn away to avoid this man whose skin had been eaten away by leprosy. But to Francis's surprise, he was suddenly filled with compassion and turned towards the man. He dismounted his horse, gave the man money, embraced him warmly, and kissed him tenderly on the lips. He literally put his lips on that which disgusted him most. This was the watershed moment in Francis's spiritual life. When he got back on his horse and looked around, he no longer saw the man. He eventually came to understand that it was Jesus Christ himself whom he had kissed.

St. Francis later wrote, "This is how God inspired me, Brother Francis, to embark upon a life of penance. When I was in sin, the sight of lepers nauseated me beyond measure; but then God himself led me into their company, and I had pity on them. When I had once become acquainted with them, what had previously nauseated me became a source of physical consolation for me. After that I did not wait long before leaving the world." It was soon after this encounter that Francis left his life of wealth and power, began spending time with lepers, and started his ministry.[3]

The Greek word for sin, *hamartia*, means "to miss the mark." It is quite a different understanding than the conventional modern notion of sin as a violation of a written law or, more simply, "bad behavior"—however that behavior may be defined in any given cultural context. Francis's behavior when he was "in sin" was the result of a misperception of who and where God was. In his embrace of the leper, Francis's sight was corrected. He now recognized Christ not just as a man who lived for thirty-three years, but as the indwelling Spirit of every human being, including the leper. For Francis, this Spirit extended to all creation. He came to see all people as a manifestation of the Spirit of God, or *Christ*. Although the characters

---

3. Jack Wintz, OFM. "7 Key Moments in the Life of St. Francis." *Franciscan Spirit Blog.* [online] Available at: <https://www.franciscanmedia.org/franciscan-spirit-blog/7-key-moments-in-the-life-of-st-francis> [Accessed 21 May 2022].

were different, my encounter with the transgender woman on my porch led me to the same conclusion as Francis. The leper, the transgender woman, and everyone else was a vessel for the indwelling Spirit of Christ. There were no exceptions; therefore, there was no longer anyone to disdain or avoid. Only different manifestations of Christ to love. The Apostle John calls the indwelling Spirit of Christ "the Word":

> *In the beginning was the Word, and the Word was with God, and the Word was God. He was in the beginning with God. All things came into being through Him, and apart from Him not even one thing came into being that has come into being. In Him was life, and the life was the Light of mankind. And the Light shines in the darkness, and the darkness did not grasp it.*
>
> **—JOHN 1:1–5** (NASB)

The Word, or *Christ*, is the Spirit that flows out from God and manifests all things in physical form. This is the spiritual reality, which the mystic sees. To be "in sin" is to be in *darkness* or blind to this reality. The result of this blindness is the *perception* of separateness from God and others. Sin is not a state that one consciously chooses to enter into by willful decision. It is an inevitable state of human development. The condition is not *original*; rather, it is *inevitable*. Like Francis, there must be an encounter in each person's life where this perception of separateness is corrected and sight is restored—revealing the indwelling Spirit of God in every human and all creation.

The person of Jesus incarnates this formless, expansive Spirit of God pulsing through all of creation (Christ) and distills it through one person, expressing in human form the very essence of God and ultimate reality. The life and teachings of Jesus as portrayed and mythologized in the New Testament took on a powerful symbolic spiritual meaning, which has endured for two millennia and has profoundly shaped the course of Western civilization and the world.

The following verses express the nature of Christ, revealed through Jesus:

> *For He rescued us from the domain of darkness, and transferred us to the kingdom of His beloved Son, in whom we have redemption, the forgiveness of sins. He is the image of the invisible God, the firstborn of all creation: for by Him all things were created, both in the heavens and on earth, visible and invisible, whether thrones, or dominions, or rulers, or authorities—all things have been created through Him and for Him. He is before all things, and in Him all things hold together.*

—**COLOSSIANS 1:13–17** (NASB)

Once one is aware of the truth of this reality, mainly that Christ is the imminent Spirit of God animating all of creation, a love that was once reserved only for Jesus suddenly extends boundlessly to everything: *because the fundamental essence of Christ is hidden in everything.* The person of Jesus is then the gateway, or portal, out of the darkness—the darkness of seeing divinity exclusively in Jesus and nothing else. Through the gateway of Jesus, we transfer into the *kingdom*—where we recognize Christ as the indwelling essence of everything that exists.

The Christian mystic is one who has made the leap from loving Jesus to loving everything because they see Jesus in everyone and everything else. This is the reality from which they see.

> *Only the Divine matters.*
> *And because the Divine matters,*
> *Everything matters.*

—**THOMAS KEATING**, O.C.S.O. (1923–2018)[4]

---

4. Thomas Keating, "What Matters," *The Secret Embrace* (Temple Rock Company: 2018), poem VIII.

CHAPTER 2

Finding Christ in the Bible

With that foundation laid, let me describe how I now read the Bible, which is important for understanding the rest of this book. My hermeneutic is based on the theory that the character of God has never changed, but that the human understanding of God's character has. This evolution of human consciousness concerning God is summed up succinctly by Brian Zahnd:

> *God is like Jesus. God has always been like Jesus. There has never been a time when God was not like Jesus. We haven't always known this, but now we do.*
>
> **—BRIAN ZAHND**[5]

Zahnd is emphasizing here that we should understand the Bible as a narrative of human consciousness struggling to understand God—and often misunderstanding. The human understanding of God matures throughout the text until the invisible nature of God is finally revealed through Jesus. Jesus "upgrades" our understanding

---

5. Brian Zahnd is the pastor at Word of Life Church in St. Joseph, Missouri. Used with permission.

of what God is like, so that we can correct our mistaken perceptions about God.

To put it plainly, I look for Jesus in every Bible story—even if the story says nothing about Jesus. As I said in the previous chapter, Christ is the imminent Spirit of God animating all of creation. Christ has been present since the beginning, breathing creation into life and sustaining it. Christ was the Spirit that animated Jesus's life. We can understand Christ with nuance, in that, although Christ has always been present, the exact nature of Christ was not fully revealed until the incarnation of Jesus. Jesus's temporal incarnation on earth gives concrete definition to the nature of Christ. Jesus makes visible the Christ which is invisible. Jesus and Christ are paradoxically distinct and also one. An imperfect metaphor for this is thinking of air in a balloon. The air (representing Christ) is constantly present, but by filling a balloon (representing Jesus), we can better understand the properties and characteristics of the air (Christ). The balloon (Jesus) temporarily embodies the air (Christ), and through that embodiment, we realize that the air (Christ) has always been here and will continue to be. Forgive the unsanctimonious metaphor, but I hope it helps illustrate the distinction.

The purpose of Jesus is to reveal the true character of God. So, in every Bible story, including Old Testament stories, I look for the character who most closely resembles the Spirit of Christ as revealed by Jesus. *Sometimes the character who most resembles Christ is not the "God" character.* I know what God is like through my personal encounter with Christ on my front porch. I know what God is like through the life of Jesus in the New Testament. *So, if the "God" character in a Bible story does not reflect the character of Jesus, then I know that the "God" character is not God.* Sometimes the "God" character in a Bible story is not Christlike and the Spirit of Christ must be found elsewhere in the story. You might be thinking, "Huh? How can the God character in the story not actually be God?" Good question. Reading the "God" character as God is indeed one way of reading Scripture. There are many other ways to read it though. Jesus's repeated formula for people devoted to their particular reading of scripture is: "You have heard it said... but I say..."

There is a big difference between what God is actually like (Jesus) and what humans *think* God is like. *When the Bible presents a depiction of God that is contrary to the exact nature of God as revealed in Jesus, I know that the depiction I'm reading is not actually God.* Rather, it is a depiction of what humans *think* God is like. Is God a vengeful tyrant who demands firstborn sons be sacrificed? *Or is God like Jesus?* Is God violent and egotistical? *Or is God like Jesus?* Does God commit genocide with floods? *Or is God like Jesus?* Does God punish people? *Or is God like Jesus?*

An example would be the story of Abraham and Isaac. When you look at the three main characters in this story—God, Abraham, and Isaac—which character looks most like Jesus? Is it the "God" character who demands a brutal child sacrifice? Or is it Isaac who is non-violent and loving towards the person who is about to murder him? I insist that Christ is revealed here in Isaac.

The human perception was, *and largely still is*, that God requires an innocent human sacrifice for the atonement of sins. In his book *What is the Bible?* Rob Bell points out that before Abraham takes Isaac up the mountain to sacrifice him to God, he says to his servants, "Stay here with the donkey while I and the boy go over there. We will worship and *then we will come back to you.*" (Genesis 22:5)[6]. Before even taking Isaac up the mountain, Abraham assures his servants that *both of them will return*. Abraham knows God does not require sacrificial killing! But he still has to act out the whole ritual up until the point of the violent ending everyone is expecting. The

---

6. Rob Bell, *What is the Bible? How an Ancient Library of Poems, Letters, and Stories Can Transform the Way You Think and Feel About Everything* (New York: HarperCollins, 2017), 110.

human mind usually needs to be shocked into the truth about God. "You have heard it said… but I say…" From the very first book of the Bible, humans with a clear knowledge of what God is really like have been saying, "You think God requires a sacrifice for the atonement of sins…but I say God is non-violent and all-merciful."

> *For I desire mercy, not sacrifice, an acknowledgment of God rather than burnt offerings.*
>
> **—HOSEA 6:6** (NIV)

Little by little, Scripture seems to nudge the human perception of God—as wrathful, violent, and punitive—towards a more loving and merciful understanding of God, as finally and fully revealed in Jesus. *It is not God who changes throughout the text; it is the human understanding of God that is shifted.* This shift is often shocking, awe-inspiring, and humiliating—especially for Christians! How else would we learn humility without realizing we had God all wrong?

Before becoming doctors, medical students must take the Hippocratic Oath in which they pledge to *"first, do no harm."* This is an act of humility which demands that doctors do not overestimate their ability to heal, or underestimate their capacity to harm. The aim is for doctors to be vigilant about the power that they hold—to strive to remain sober-minded before jumping into action. We should adopt this principle with the Bible. Can you imagine if Christians were required to take an oath to "first, do no harm" with the Bible?

I have a good friend named Jessica who, during her own questioning of the character of God in light of Jesus, found herself teaching Bible stories to children in a private Christian school. The curriculum was given to her to teach, and as she began reading old familiar Bible stories to prepare for the school lesson, she began to feel conflicted about presenting God in the unflattering light that the character was portrayed in the stories. She would often reach out to me saying, *"This version of God doesn't reflect who Jesus is."* We would then search the story to find *someone* in the text reflecting love that appeared Christ-like. It often was not the "God" character. Jessica decided to operate using the "do no harm" principle. If she couldn't find a reflection of Jesus in the story, she'd skip that part. She realized that she held the power to turn God into an angry tyrant to be feared by the children she was responsible for teaching. She was humble enough to do nothing rather than risk harming children's hearts and minds by carelessly reading the text at face value. Reading the Bible literally, like a news report, robs us of understanding its intrinsic depth of wisdom and saddles us with a rigid, fearful, and lifeless understanding of God.

> *If anyone causes one of these little ones—those who believe in me—to stumble, it would be better for them to have a large millstone hung around their neck and to be drowned in the depths of the sea.*
>
> **—MATTHEW 18:6** (NIV)

The Bible deals with life's greatest mysteries and humanity's struggle to understand, flourish, and live in harmony with mystery. The key to unlocking the depths of the Bible is in awakening to the essence of Christ as revealed in Jesus. Only then can one recognize Christ in the Bible where Jesus is not explicitly named. An accurate recognition of Christ corrects our distorted perception of God. That distorted perception is reflected over and over again by characters written about in the Bible (including the "God" character), and we risk falling into distortion with a strictly literal interpretation of the text. It is essential that a person reads the Bible through the lens of Christ, which requires an unwavering certitude in the qualities of the character of Jesus and the Spirit that animated his life. Apart from that, one will take the words of the text as impetus for violent behavior towards themselves, other humans, and creation.

> *Leave them; they are blind guides. If the blind lead the blind, both will fall into a pit.*
>
> **—MATTHEW 15:14** (NIV)

CHAPTER 3

The Anatomy of a Seed

It's important before we get farther into the book that I establish some terminology that I will use moving forward. Although it is impossible to speak of spirituality and mystery with exact precision, metaphors can provide the mind a handle by which to grasp spiritual concepts so that they can be discussed.

A major principle that eventually surfaces on the path of spiritual seeking, including within the tradition of Christianity (in contemplative and mystical paths), is the concept of the True Self and False Self. Unfortunately, this teaching is usually not found within contemporary Christianity. My personal feeling is that this is not a willful omission. Rather, many mainstream religious teachers and adherents are unaware of it or do not understand it. The Bible alludes to this spiritual reality in many of its metaphors, but I feel it is necessary now to describe this principle of spirituality explicitly in order for humanity to move forward together. Spiritual ignorance continues to foster unnecessary personal and global division, which is unsustainable. Through advancements in psychology, we can now assert that the principle of the True Self and False Self is not simply an ambiguous spiritual theory. Rather, it has increasingly become essential in the science of understanding human development, trauma, neurosis, and psychological healing.

In the field of psychology, the human psyche is defined as containing all elements of a person's mind and soul, conscious and unconscious. The different parts of the psyche are not physically concrete like anatomical parts of the brain, but it is necessary to label them in order to work with them. There are various labels that refer to the True Self: *soul, essence, essential nature, inner child, etc.* Likewise, the False Self might also be called: *ego, flesh, dualistic mind, egoic personality, persona, mask, etc.* For simplicity, I will use the terms True Self and False Self in this book.

Following my mystical encounter with the transgender woman on my porch, I began voraciously seeking literature that would help me make sense of my shifting perceptions about religion and spirituality. I stumbled upon an obscure commentary written by Maurice Nicoll. It opens with an entry entitled *Letter to Mr. Bush.*[7] In his letter, Nicoll describes the psychological and spiritual stages of human development corresponding to the life cycle of an acorn. From then on, I could not get that metaphor out of my head, as a reflection of what I knew to be true of my experience. That inspiration planted a seed in me that grew into what was eventually this book.

He presented another parable to them, saying, "The kingdom of heaven is like a mustard seed, which a man took and sowed in his field; and this is smaller than all other seeds, but when it is fully grown, it is larger than the garden plants and becomes a tree, so that the birds of the air come and nest in its branches."

—MATTHEW 13:31–32 (NASB)

---

7. Maurice Nicoll, "Letter to Mr. Bush; March 27, 1941." *Psychological Commentaries on the Teaching of Gurdjieff and Ouspensky, Volume 1* (York Beach: Red Wheel/Weiser, LLC, 1996), 1–7.

In this metaphor, Jesus is describing the concept of the True Self and False Self. In order to understand the metaphor, it's essential to understand the anatomy of a seed. If you were asked the question, "What does a seed look like?", most likely you would picture the round, smooth, intact object that you can hold between your index finger and thumb. The outside of the seed is, in fact, only one part of the seed. But it is the part that our brains identify as the *whole* seed. In reality, there are more parts below the surface. The anatomy of a seed is a useful way of envisioning the True Self and False Self.

When opened, the seed actually contains an embryo within the shell. In order for the seed to grow into a tree, the outside shell—the part of the seed that we identify as the whole seed—actually has to break open and die. It is the embryo inside of the shell that then takes root and, once the roots are firmly established, grows into a tree. This is illustrated in the diagram below. The seed coat, or outer shell, represents the False Self, and the embryonic seed leaf and root represents the True Self.

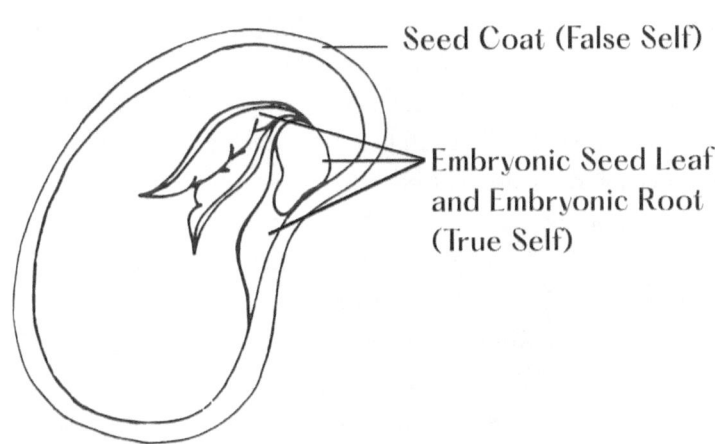

Seed Coat (False Self)

Embryonic Seed Leaf and Embryonic Root (True Self)

The seed's process of germination mirrors what must happen in order for a person to access their True Self—which Jesus calls *"the kingdom of heaven"* in the parable of the mustard seed. The tree on which a seed originates is like a *first womb* from which the seed grows, and it symbolizes God who gives *birth* to all creation. The seed experiences itself as one with the tree, a part of the whole. This is a child's state of consciousness, experiencing itself as one with its mother. The seed, or fruit, must then *fall* from the tree. This is a good and necessary process for life to continue and for each seed to fulfill its potential destiny of becoming a tree all its own. Like the seed falling from the tree, a child's consciousness eventually shifts from experiencing reality as connected to the source of its existence (God, represented by the tree), to experiencing itself as *separate from God* (the seed fallen from the tree). The human mind now identifies itself with the outer shell, experiencing itself as separate and fallen from its source. The conscious mind is unaware that what it is, the seed, is a self-contained tree. The source of its life and potential growth is inside the outer shell. *The True Self (embryo) is hidden inside the False Self (outer shell).* The human being (represented by the seed) senses deep down that their purpose is to become a tree. But they don't know how to accomplish this. They only see the outside of themselves. They identify completely with their outer shell, their False Self, and lack awareness of the True Self hidden within. Consequently, the False Self becomes a personality which strives to imitate the potential of the True Self. But because it is an imitation of the True Self and not the real thing, the False Self, or egoic personality, becomes inflated and self-loathing.

This state of consciousness is what the Bible refers to as *sin*. In Chapter One, *The Christian of the Future*, I mentioned that the Greek word for sin, *hamartia*, means "to miss the mark." The state of sin arises when the False Self is aiming to realize itself as a potential "tree" through an inflated, egoic personality. The result of this striving leads to addictive, compulsive, and narcissistic behaviors in an effort to emulate the True Self. Until a human becomes conscious of the fact that they are, in fact, *not* the False Self, *not* the outer shell, they will continue to suffer in this state of sin, or missing the mark, because they will attempt to become a tree while circumventing the process required to grow into a tree. The False Self is like a little seed gazing up at the majestic trees around it, either pretending it is already a tree when it is not, or self-loathing over the apparent impossibility of becoming one. The False Self is ignorant that it contains within itself the keys for transformation.

Like a seed, the False Self (outer shell) must be buried in the ground, which is like a *second womb*. It is from this second womb that one can be spiritually *born again*. Once buried, the False Self can begin to break open and subsequently die, allowing the True Self (embryo) to first take root in the ground and secondly sprout back up to the surface and continue its growth into a tree.

It is important to back up and note that the embryo, or True Self, cannot survive without the outer shell, or False Self. The treacherous journey from the fruiting on the original tree—to the fall to the ground—through the brutal elements of nature—and finally burial in the ground—would not be possible without the outer shell. The embryo would never be able to complete its necessary journey without the protection of the outer shell. Likewise, the flourishing of the True Self would not be possible without the development and subsequent protection of the False Self. It is only once the True Self is ready for *rebirth in the second womb* that the False Self no longer serves a purpose and must die and be buried. This is the process of *dying to (False) Self.* Indeed, the state of sin, represented by the False Self (outer shell), is actually a natural and necessary state of development, without which we would not survive to realize our full potential and experience grace in God. What an antidote to guilt and shame! We can surrender the False Self at the proper time, understanding its purpose which frees us from self-loathing. The English mystic, Julian of Norwich, calls sin necessary:

It was necessary that there should be sin; but all shall be well,
and all shall be well, and all manner of things shall be well.
                  —**JULIAN OF NORWICH**[8] (c. 1342–c. 1416)[9]

This process of dying to the (False) Self is the *Way* described by
Jesus and visually represented in his crucifixion, burial, and resurrec-
tion. Through this cruciform process, the human's consciousness is
restored to wholeness, identified as the True Self grounded and sus-
tained by God and in harmony with all of nature. The consciousness
now identifies itself as a *child of God* or offspring of the Tree, growing
in the likeness of the source from which it fell. It recognizes that this
was always its identity, and that it was simply unaware of this truth
before. This misplaced identity—this identification with the False
Self, this unawareness of the True Self, this "missing the mark"—is
sin. It is not an *original* state of consciousness as most of Christianity
has come to believe through the doctrine of original sin. The term
"original sin" is not found in the Bible. The idea was proposed by St.
Augustine hundreds of years after Jesus. The Bible actually begins
with a declaration in Genesis 1 and 2 that we are "good…good…
good…good…good…*very good.*" I will delve into original sin fur-
ther in Chapter Twenty-Three, *Original Sin.*

Fr. Richard Rohr, OFM is a Franciscan priest whose work and
teaching have been extremely illuminating for me. He names the
pattern of spiritual transformation, which begins with our individ-
ual and collective goodness. He emphasizes humanity's Original
Goodness as inherent and asserts the potential humans have to real-
ize our true nature and let it flourish:

---

8. Julian of Norwich, *Revelations of Divine Love.* Edited by Grace Warrack (London:
Methuen & Company, 1901), 56.

9. Julian of Norwich is considered to be one of the greatest English mystics and the first
known female writer in English.

From the very beginning, faith, hope, and love are planted deep within our nature [the embryo]—indeed they are our very nature. Christian life is simply a matter of becoming who we already are.

—FR. RICHARD ROHR[10]

Identification with the False Self, or the state of sin, is a necessary and unavoidable level of consciousness that serves as a vehicle for the survival and development of life. However, once the shell of the False Self has served its purpose, resisting the call to die becomes detrimental to the birth of the True Self. If the False Self (outer shell) is not crucified, or *sacrificed*, the True Self (embryo) cannot resurrect and become a tree. Apart from this process, a human soul is *lost*—like a seed blown by the wind, unaware of its true identity and purpose, and unable to fulfill its destiny.

Having now understood the concept of the True Self and False Self, read the words of St. Paul in 1 Corinthians 15 (The Message). Imagine the False Self when he talks about the seed and the True Self when he discusses the plant:

Some skeptic is sure to ask, "Show me how resurrection works. Give me a diagram; draw me a picture. What does this 'resurrection body' look like?" If you look at this question closely, you realize how absurd it is. There are no diagrams for this kind of thing. We do have a parallel experience in gardening. You plant a "dead" seed; soon there is a flourishing plant. There is no visual likeness between seed and plant. You could never guess what a tomato would look like by looking at a tomato seed. What we plant in the soil and what grows out of it don't look anything alike. The dead body that we bury in the ground and

10. Richard Rohr, *The Universal Christ: How a Forgotten Reality Can Change Everything We See, Hope for, and Believe* (New York: Convergent, 2019), 65.

the resurrection body that comes from it will be dramatically different.

You will notice that the variety of bodies is stunning. Just as there are different kinds of seeds, there are different kinds of bodies—humans, animals, birds, fish—each unprecedented in its form. You get a hint at the diversity of resurrection glory by looking at the diversity of bodies not only on earth but in the skies—sun, moon, stars—all these varieties of beauty and brightness. And we're only looking at pre-resurrection "seeds"— who can imagine what the resurrection "plants" will be like!

This image of planting a dead seed and raising a live plant is a mere sketch at best, but perhaps it will help in approaching the mystery of the resurrection body—but only if you keep in mind that when we're raised, we're raised for good, alive forever! The corpse that's planted is no beauty, but when it's raised, it's glorious. Put in the ground weak, it comes up powerful. The seed sown is natural; the seed grown is supernatural—same seed, same body, but what a difference from when it goes down in physical mortality to when it is raised up in spiritual immortality!

—1 CORINTHIANS 15:35-44 (MSG)

Acknowledgements

At the beginning, I dedicated this book to my steadfast friends. I began to name a few of them for supporting me over the past few years through my ups and down and life's difficulties, but there are too many friends whom I love dearly, and I do not want to leave anyone out. I realize how lucky I am to say that. If you're one of the people in my life who listens to me process my thoughts out loud at random times, gets my humor, laughs at my jokes, and solves the world's problems with me—thank you. My life is rich because of you!

Thank you to Jonathan Foster and Thomas Jay Oord at SacraSage Press for helping me bring *Eat the Dirt* into the world. Jonathan, I have felt a kindred spirit in you since we first spoke on your podcast, and I'm glad we got to work on this book of poems together.

Thank you to Rafael Polendo for again taking my creative vision and turning it into true art that graces the cover. I think most people are buying my books for your cover art!

Thank you to Achmad Nuryawan for the care you took to create the interior illustrations. You are a brilliant artist who brought my visions to life.

Thank you to Jessica Condrey for grounding me when I get in my head and encouraging me to press on with my weird ideas. Your feedback is invaluable to me!

Jared, thank you for all your support in making this book a reality. I'm so grateful for your encouragement in my endeavors.

Norah, Jacob, and Florence—I simply love being your mom. Each year that you get older is a joy for me to witness. Mothering you three has easily been the most joyful experience of my life. I love the people you are, the dreams you are dreaming, and watching you grow into humans I continuously want to be around.

About the Author

Heather Hamilton lives near Atlanta, Georgia. She received her B.A. in Journalism from Georgia State University and spent many years doing video production before discovering her love of writing. In 2023, she released her debut book, *Returning to Eden: A Field Guide for the Spiritual Journey*. She has been featured on numerous podcast, television, and radio programs to discuss Christian symbolism and mythology.

To keep in touch with Heather or inquire about speaking or Spiritual Direction, please visit

https://www.ReturningtoEden.com

You can also follow her on social media at:

heatherhamiltonauthor.substack.com
www.instagram.com/heatherhamilton1
www.facebook.com/heatherhamiltonauthor

www.ingramcontent.com/pod-product-compliance
Lightning Source LLC
Chambersburg PA
CBHW031427120626
46545CB00006B/2298